This yearbook belongs to...

....

I can't wait to show you all the exciting
stuff that happened this past year!

This Esme

YEARBOOK

Published by DJ Murphy (Publishers) Ltd, Marlborough House, Headley Road, Grayshott, Surrey GU26 6LG

WHO DID WHAT IN THIS ESME YEARBOOK 2021
Esme Higgs
Contributors Helen Barker-Benfield, Tilly Berendt, Hollie Bladen, Jo Brown, Megan Hurley, Bethany Searby, Lianne Tadd and Hollie's mum
Art Editor Sarah Garland
Designer Lizzi Porter
Lifestyle photographers Lucy Merrell, Jon Stroud, David Higgs
Photo credits Mitch Gunn/shutterstock.com klauscook/shutterstock.com, singkam/shutterstock.com
Publishing Director Zoe Cannon
Commercial Director Abigail Cannon
Managing Director Kate Austin

This Esme Yearbook is produced under license by DJ Murphy (Publishers) Ltd.
© Copyright DJ Murphy (Publishers) Ltd.

Printed by Graphicom via dell'Industria – 36100 Vicenza, Italy

ISBN 978-1-913787-00-4

This Esme

Meet the MENAGERIE

Each year it feels as though our herd gets a little bigger, so here's an update on all our gorgeous animals!

CASPER

Being my first horse, Casper has taught me sooo much! He hadn't done a lot when I got him and was really spooky, but together we've learned loads and achieved more than we ever imagined. He really loves jumping and heading to the beach for a blast along the water's edge.

Vital stats
Height: 15hh
Born: 2006
Colour: Grey
Breed: Connemara

THE CHICKENS

I've wanted chickens for a long time, and finally for my 18th birthday I got Snickers, Bounty, Mars and Milky. They're all the same age – which is really important to make sure that they get on well with each other and don't squabble too much. The chickens are a mixture of breeds – Bounty's a Blue Haze, Milky a Light Sussex, Snickers is a Maran and Mars is a Rhode Rock. I love them all, but I definitely have a soft spot for Snickers who always comes to see me when I'm mucking out.

MICKEY

I have grown up a lot since we got Mickey when I was eight years old, but he's still a huge part of my life. We did everything together from my first Pony Club camp to mounted games competitions. When I outgrew Mickey, I couldn't imagine life without him, so we decided to retire Mickey here on the farm.

Vital stats
Height: 13hh
Born: 1999
Colour: Cremello
Breed: Unknown

JOEY

My journey with Joey has only just begun. It took me months of searching to find my new horse, but with Joey I just knew he was the perfect fit for me. He's so affectionate and tries super-hard with his schooling. I'm really excited about our future together.

Vital stats
Height: 16hh
Born: 2014
Colour: Dapple grey
Breed: Thoroughbred x Warmblood

THE DONKEYS

Willow, Bruno and Toby have lived here since before I was even born, so I can't imagine life without them. Willow's the only female equine we have and she's definitely the sassiest, although she's calmed down a lot in her old age and really enjoys a good cuddle. Our two jack donkeys are Bruno who's brown and Toby who's black. Toby lacks confidence on his own, so you tend to find him waiting in the wings as the others vie for attention.

BARN
HACKS

Here are some of my tips to stream-line your yard routine – perfect to give you extra time with your pony!

1. Use a dandy brush or a special hair removal comb to help get rid of the hair stuck to the inside of your saddle pads before you wash them.

2. Use leftover drinking water to soak haynets or wash your fave pony's tail. It's a great way to save water and it'll save you time waiting for buckets to fill, too!

This Esme

White hairs seem to get everywhere!

3. Use a watering can to wash your fave pony rather than the hose. It'll save loads of water, which is great for the environment.

4. Make sure you store your rugs and numnahs super-neatly – mine are colour co-ordinated, but you can order them however you want. When you take one out, make sure you put it back how you found it – this will save you loads of time when you need to grab something in a hurry!

6. Fitting a door chain to your stable is a really good idea, because it means you can pop in and out of your pony's stable without having to unbolt the door each time. It also improves ventilation and helps to keep your stable cool in the summer months. »

5. Tie some baler twine through the handle of your hoof picks and hang them up in accessible places. Have one on the yard, one outside your pony's stable and another in the tack room so there's always one to hand, whenever you need it!

7. Don't go anywhere on the yard empty handed! Stuff always needs moving, so take fewer trips by being one step ahead and thinking about what needs to be where for later.

8. Fill your haynets in advance – if you have enough you could even do them for the whole week! This saves you loads of time on busy mornings and also helps you plan your next delivery of hay.

9. Apply sun cream to your pony's muzzle if he has pink skin which burns easily. I use one with a high SPF which is suitable for children as it's kind to Mickey's skin.

Saving time means more time with your pony!

10. Rolling up your leadrope after you use it will help to keep your tack room neat, and it'll be easy to grab in an emergency. To do this, hold the rope just below the clip and double it up so that you have a double section of rope approximately 20cm long. Wrap the excess rope around the doubled up section until you get to the end, then thread your rope through the loop at the bottom.

11. If you don't have time to give your tack a thorough clean every time you ride, save time by rinsing off your pony's bit and just wiping the areas which get really dirty, such as the flash strap or girth. You can give your tack a thorough clean at the weekend when you do have time. See my guide on page 38 to help you.

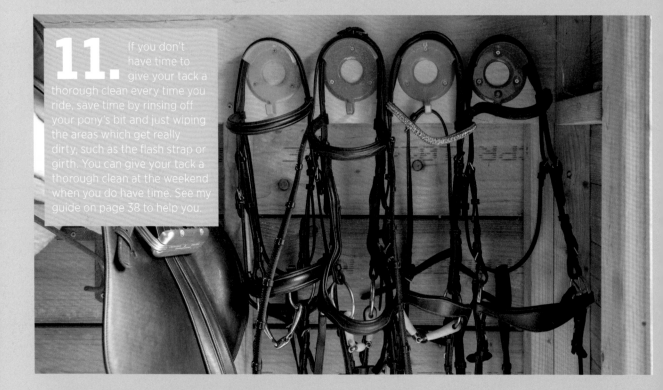

12. If you know you're going to be busy, prepare your pony's feeds ready for the evening and following day – I do this for my Mum when I'm away.

13. Pop a tennis ball in your pony's water buckets and trough to stop them freezing in the winter so he'll always have plenty to drink.

This Esme

—1

—90

14. Measure your jump wings and mark heights you often use with coloured tape or a marker pen so you can quickly see where to set the poles for each session.

11

JANUARY & FEBRUARY

The weather may be a bit chill, but quality time with your pony is still the best! Follow my guide for a fab start to the new year...

Winter evenings are a perfect opportunity to start thinking about the year ahead – why don't you create a list of goals you want to achieve with your pony? Think about what you might like to learn, the places you'd like to visit and the competitions you'd like to ride at. For example, you might want to qualify for The Pony Club Championships, learn to ride a flying change or meet your horsey hero at Hickstead. By writing a list, you can plan your qualifiers, chat to your instructor and book your tickets.

If you're daydreaming about a bit of fun in the sun, tune in to the Winter Equestrian Festival (WEF), which takes place over 12 weeks from early January, and attracts some of the world's best riders to south Florida. It's glamorous and exciting, with tons of rings offering round-the-clock entertainment – and even if you can't persuade your parents to book a holiday in West Palm Beach, you can catch most of the action from the world's biggest horse show through the WEF livestream.

Celebrate Valentine's Day with the love of your life – your fave pony, of course! You can make your own treats by grating an apple and a carrot into a mixing bowl, adding a cup of molasses, two and a half cups of rolled oats and two tablespoons of vegetable oil. Simply spread the mixture over a parchment-lined baking tray or shape into cute little hearts, bake for 40 mins at 150°C, then pop in the fridge for a few hours to set.

Keep your riding sessions super-fun and active by using poles, cones and barrels to play mounted games with your yard friends. You'll find loads of great ideas on YouTube, and there's no chance of getting cold when you're trying to win a sack race!

Wintery days call for inside jobs, such as an overhaul of your grooming kit or tack box. Give your brushes a good wash and set aside any empty spray bottles ready to be refilled – it's way cheaper and much kinder to the planet than throwing them out!

I love an overhaul!

"The weather outside may be dreary, but time with your pony is always cheery"

ALL ABOUT Joey

Get to know the newest member of my herd, Joey

NEED TO KNOW:

Name: Joey
Colour: Dapple grey
Breed: TB x WB
Height: 16hh
Sex: Gelding
Owned Since: March 2020
Hashtag: #JoeyThisEsme
Matchy-matchy colour: Green
Cheekiest habit: He kicks the door if you aren't quick enough making his breakfast!

" Joey is so affectionate and loves nothing more than a great big cuddle "

Did you know?
Just like Mickey and Casper, Joey's a mud magnet – good job I've had years of grooming practice!

Did you know?
Joey and Casper share the same size rugs, boots and headcollars.

Getting used to Joey's long stride!

A STAR IN THE MAKING

Joey wasn't quite six when I got him, but we're ready to grow together and achieve our goals. He hasn't affiliated before, so he's a bit of a blank canvas. I chose Joey because he ticked all my boxes, and his personality and temperament are amazing – I've never known a more affectionate horse. He loves cuddles, kisses and scratches. I fell in love with him straight away and I'm hoping you guys will, too. Joey gets on so well with the other ponies – he and Casper love giving each other a really good groom. When Joey and Mickey first met, Mickey couldn't help but squeal at him - but now Mickey acts like his shadow and is always following him around the field.

Joey has an excellent jump, with plenty of scope to go higher in the future. His old owners did some showjumping with him and had planned to event. It's really exciting and I can't wait to see where our future takes us.

Did you know?
Joey finds the film camera really interesting and activates Giraffe Joey mode whenever he sees it.

JOEY'S FIRST FEW DAYS

Why I love
XC SCHOOLING

Casper's most favourite thing in the world is going cross-country, and with a brand-new all-weather facility just down the road from where we live, we can practise all year round!

The right gear

When you ride cross-country it's really important that you and your pony have the right tack and clothing. Here's my essential kit list:

For me
Safety helmet – one which doesn't have a fixed peak
Body protector
Gloves
Riding boots
Plus, XC is always a good excuse to wear a cool matchy-matchy base layer

For Casper
Saddle
Bridle
XC boots
Overreach boots
Saddle pad (preferably to match my baselayer)

XC is fast-paced and fun!

BEFORE YOU START

It's super-important to warm your pony up properly before jumping cross-country fences. Not only will this loosen up his muscles, it'll make sure he's really listening to you and responding to your leg. With Casper, I like to walk around the warm-up arena and let him have a good look at what's going on. He can be quite spooky sometimes so it's good to give him plenty of time to relax. Next I have a trot and canter on both reins. Then the real work starts and I ask Casper for some longer strides in canter then shorter, more bouncy, strides. I ride lots of transitions so that I know he's being responsive and will come back to a trot if I ask him to, or can take a few longer strides between fences if the distance is long.

Before I tackle any cross-country fences I like to pop Casper over a cross-pole a couple of times so I can see how he's feeling that day. »

ACING CROSS-COUNTRY FENCES

While it might seem a bit daunting to jump a fence that doesn't fall down if you knock it, many horses – like Casper – actually prefer natural obstacles. However, it's important to ride positively when you're going cross-country. Make sure your pony has a forward canter with plenty of energy and that you're looking up and ahead to the fence. When you get four or five strides out, sit a little deeper in the saddle and ride positively to the fence, then gently fold as your pony takes off.

UP AND DOWN STEPS

A lot of cross-country fences are jumped from a fast pace, but jumping down steps in particular requires control. I like to bring Casper back to a trot five or six strides out from a step to give him time to see what the question is and work out how to tackle it. I keep my shoulders back and sit up tall, making sure that my leg is on even though I've asked Casper to slow down. When Casper jumps off the step I allow a little with my reins so he can use his head and neck to help him balance, and lean back slightly so I don't overbalance forward onto his shoulders.

Jumping up steps requires a bouncy canter with lots of energy. Casper really likes to gallop on when we go cross-country, so I sit tall, bring my shoulders back and ask him to wait. Then I ride positively to the fence, being sure to fold forward as he jumps up. When your pony jumps up a bank out of water it's even more important to ride with lots of power – but not speed – as the water provides resistance which will make it harder for your pony to leap out.

JUMPING SKINNIES

Cross country-courses are often a test of your accuracy as well as your pony's bravery and fitness. Skinny fences are harder to ride than standard jumps as it's easier for a horse to run out to one side. When I'm approaching a skinny fence with Casper I like to bring him back to more of a showjumping canter and concentrate on approaching the fence in a super-straight line. That way I'm giving him every opportunity to clear the fence.

Super-straight over a skinny!

IN AND OUT OF WATER

Some horses can be really unsure of jumping into water, and if you think about it from an evolutionary perspective, they've every right to! I'm very fortunate with Casper that he really enjoys water of all kinds, including swimming in the sea. Even so, I always like to walk him into a water jump for the first time when we're training as it gives him lots of confidence.

As I ride towards the water, I sit up with my shoulders back and ride positively. When your pony takes his first few steps into the water give him lots of praise. Some horses aren't keen on the water splashing their tummy so make sure you ride with a secure position, too! Once they're really comfortable walking in and out you can try a trot – and if your horse loves water as much as Casper does, why not try jumping in and out?

15 SECONDS OF FAME

TikTok

While I'm best known for being a Youtuber, I have a lot of fun on my TikTok channel. Here's my guide to setting up your own TikTok profile

Need to know
TikTok accounts are public by default – but you can adjust your privacy settings by tapping the three dots in the top right corner of your profile.

Did someone say glow up?

Need to know
You need to be 13 to create a TikTok account and you should check with your parents or guardians first.

PERFECT PROFILE

Try to come up with a unique username then add a bio and a profile picture. Keep it snappy and fun – mine's @this_esme and my bio says 'Yeah, I'm that horse girl from YouTube' 🐴. When you choose an image for your profile, make sure it's a really clear photo that works small. Tiny details will get totally lost.

TURN UP THE VOLUME

TikTok started life as a lip-syncing app and its musical roots can still be heard loud and clear. Choosing the right soundtrack is a huge part of creating TikTok content so it might be time to expand your musical repertoire! You can browse TikTok's Spotify-esque streaming menu of artists for inspiration. Sometimes I hear a piece of music, or an audio clip, and I just know the lyrics will make a really funny video – like the *This is my family* @**STEEERLING** clip I use to illustrate Mickey's amazing half unicorn, half pig personality! 🦄🐷 I've even been known to sing my own made-up songs #cringe!

CHALLENGE ACCEPTED!

TikTokers unite for #challenges and you'll find the songs associated with these in the music streaming menu. There's plenty to choose from – just hit the search button to see what's trending and have a go yourself. As well as challenges there are really cute audio clips like #barncheck you can use to introduce all your fave horses to your followers.

Rating my horse throughout the day ✨

TRANSITIONS

So you've mastered walk, trot and canter on your pony – now it's time to master transitions TikTok style! Zoom in, slip, scroll, horizon and rotate will all add energy to a video between scenes without distracting from the story. If you're recording in TikTok, tap *effects* and then *transitions* to open the effects panel and try a few to see how they look.

HAVE FUN

TikTok is more about entertainment than any other social media platform. It's full of dancing, lip-syncing and things to make you laugh, so try and keep your posts light-hearted, super-fun and a bit silly!

Puzzle fun

WORDSEARCH

Can you find all the words hidden in this puzzle?

H	Y	R	S	E	S	V	O	E	M	A	R	S	I
M	R	S	S	K	C	A	H	N	S	T	N	E	S
W	T	B	A	R	N	T	O	U	R	I	M	P	O
Y	N	R	B	B	I	L	T	O	C	S	L	O	W
C	U	A	O	E	O	S	B	K	E	N	O	L	X
M	O	T	U	O	U	R	E	E	E	B	W	E	O
O	C	A	N	O	M	R	M	P	D	A	P	W	B
O	S	C	T	H	S	I	C	T	J	Y	T	O	E
R	S	H	Y	O	C	L	L	I	U	I	P	R	S
K	O	A	A	K	J	J	E	K	M	I	U	K	R
C	R	E	E	O	T	B	M	T	Y	I	W	U	O
K	C	A	R	T	D	N	U	O	S	I	O	Q	H
T	M	I	L	T	I	D	E	K	T	T	L	E	E
B	O	H	B	E	Y	U	T	U	O	Y	G	B	L

○ Barn tour
○ Glow up
○ Soundtrack
○ Snickers
○ Mars

○ Milky
○ Bounty
○ Edit
○ Polework
○ Hacks

○ Cross-country
○ TikTok
○ Horsebox
○ DIY
○ Esme

Turn to page 100 for the answers!

SPOT THE DIFFERENCE

Can you spot all seven differences in the bottom picture?

> **"** Seeing the world's best competing at such a stunning venue was an incredible experience! **"**

Make a cute carrot treat holder

What's better than a carrot? A carrot that's full of horse treats!

You all know how much Mickey loves the sight of his treat tin, but sometimes I like to make the horses little surprises like these! And the best thing is, they're super-easy to make. Fill them with treats for your pony or even marshmallows and hot chocolate powder for your mates!

What you'll need:
- Orange card
- Template from page 101
- Green ribbon
- Scissors
- Ruler
- Glue
- Hole punch
- Pencil
- Treats

Top tip

I have to closely monitor Mickey's weight so I always opt for low-sugar snacks for him.

let's get started

1 Cut out the template, or trace it onto a spare piece of paper that you can cut up.

2 Carefully draw around the template onto your piece of orange card.

3 Cut out the shape, being careful to include all the tabs. Then use your hole punch to make a hole in each of the rounded tabs.

4 Use a ruler to help you make clean folds along all of the dotted lines.

5 Glue along the tab, then stick the carrot together. Leave to dry.

6 Fill your carrot treat holder with whatever goodies you want and secure the top with the green ribbon.

This Esme

"*You all know how much Mickey loves the sight of his treat tin*"

MARCH & APRIL

The spring grass is growing, winter fluff is shedding – and your pony is probably feeling extra cheeky!

After your winter tidying spree, you probably need to stock up on a few essentials before all the shows get underway. Make a list of what you need and do some online bargain-hunting! ☑

The Longines Global Champions Tour takes the very top-level showjumping to some awsome locations – don't miss the showjumping season opener at the beginning of March, which transports you to glamorous Doha in Qatar, followed by sunny Mexico City and then Miami Beach in April. 1.60m fences right by the surf? Count me in! ☑

Beautiful bluebells start to peek through in early April, and if you're lucky enough to have access to hacking paths through the woods, you'll probably see thick carpets of them by the middle of the month. They don't stick around for long, so make sure you get plenty of photos when you're out and about with your pony! ☑

The first CCI5* of the year takes place from 22–25 April, and the Land Rover Kentucky Three-Day Event is NOT to be missed! Catch all the action on USEF Network's streaming service, or if you're lucky enough to go in person, pick a spot at the Head of the Lake and get ready to snap some mega shots for your Insta! ☑

Plan a beach ride with your yard pals. This is the perfect time to do it, as many beaches have specific hours for horses, and once summer hits it can be tricky to access them. ☑

Sudden sunshine is the perfect opportunity to give your fave pony a makeover – and he'll appreciate your efforts in helping him shed his itchy winter woollies! Give him a thorough scrub, and pull or trim his mane and tail, feathers and bridlepath for a polished look. ☑

Don't just store your pony's winter rugs away without a second thought – check for any rips or holes and send them off to be washed, reproofed and repaired so they're good as new for next winter. ☑

Enjoy a blast on the beach!

" There's something truly magical about spring time "

MUD *Monster*

Top tip

Take a before and after photo so your followers can see how you transformed your muddy pony into a unicorn!

Find out how I transform Mickey from grubby to gorgeous in five easy steps!

1. FOOT PERFECT

I always start a grooming sesh by picking out Mickey's feet. I use a hoof pick to remove mud and stones, then brush off any loose dirt that's left over. I leave the hoof oil until later, though, or all the hair I brush off can stick to it!

Work from heel to toe

2. SCRUB IT OUT

Next, I grab my trusty mitt – but you could use a rubber curry comb – and scrub the dry mud off Mickey's body. Remember, it's always best to wait until the mud dries before you try and brush it.

Top tip

If your pony has super-sensitive skin you might have to use your body brush rather than a dandy brush, and give the rubber curry comb a miss.

3. BRUSHED OFF

I use a dandy brush to remove ingrained dirt from Mickey's coat. Using a short, flicking, motion I work from his neck to his quarters. Then I use a body brush to get rid of any grease or loose dirt that's leftover. »

4. MANE ATTRACTION

Now it's time to tackle Mickey's mane and tail! I like to get rid of the worst of the mud with a brush then give it a good spray with detangler. This helps me comb through Mickey's hair without pulling it too hard and hurting him.

Mickey has such a thick tail

5. FINISHING TOUCHES

Using a damp sponge, I give Mickey's eyes and nose a quick wipe – always use a different sponge for each. Finally I pop some hoof conditioner on his hooves. Then it's time to take that 'after' photo for Insta!

Top tip

Not all hoof oils are just to make your pony look mega smart, lots of them help keep hooves strong and healthy, too.

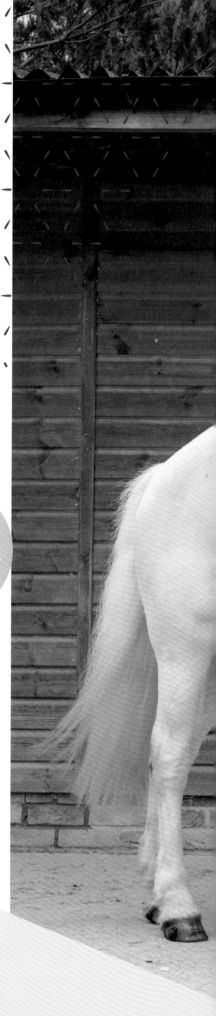

"Mickey loves being brushed, it must feel like a massage"

FIT TO RIDE

There are times when I'm working and don't get a chance to ride for days at a time, so I need a workout solution that I can do anywhere

The three main areas we need to focus on to get riding fit are stamina, suppleness and strength. For lots of us, just looking after our horses keeps us in good shape, whether it's a walk to the paddock, carrying heavy water buckets or mucking out.

As I began my search for Joey, I became aware that a bigger horse would require more stamina and core strength than I was used to, so I developed my own fitness plan.

Top tip

It's really important to stay hydrated whenever you're exercising.

Running

I got into running last year when Brooke asked me to do a 5km charity run. I thought it would be easy, but after a session on the treadmill at the gym I realised I needed to do more cardiovascular work.

I started with the couch to 5K training plan, which I found easy to follow. You run three times a week and it starts with a 25-minute run and walk, which I could do from my doorstep. While it can seem like I spend all my time out on the yard with the horses, a lot of my day is actually spent sitting at my desk editing videos – so now I use running to break up my day.

While my main reason for running is to stay fit for riding, I also find it's a great way to relax and it gives me the headspace to come up with new ideas for videos.

A great 2-in-1 exercise

Quad stretch

Stand on one leg and lift the other foot behind you so that you can grab your foot with your hand. Make sure that your knees are touching and you keep your chest up with your hips pushed forward. Don't worry if you can't get your foot to touch your bum, the focus of this exercise is on stretching your quad muscle. Keeping your hips forward will mean you'll also get a good stretch through your hip flexors. Hold the stretch for around 30 seconds and then repeat on the other side.

Top tip

You can hold the wall or a fence post to keep you steady if needed.

Hamstring stretch

Stand with your feet hip-width apart and take a step forward with one foot. Flex your foot up and bend through your hips. Keep your front leg straight as you slightly bend your back knee. Feel the stretch through your hamstring as you hold for 20–30 seconds, before switching to the other side and repeating the stretch.

Top tip

Doing this exercise with your hands against a wall will help keep your body vertical and increase the stretch through your calf.

Breathe into the stretch

Calf stretch

Stand with your feet together and take a big step forward with one leg. Keeping your body as upright as possible, lean into your front knee while trying to keep your back heel on the floor. Hold this position for 20–30 seconds before changing to the other side.

Joey is the most affectionate horse I've ever owned. I can't wait for what the future holds for us.

Make Rosette cookies

Winning a rosette is such a good feeling, but an edible cookie version is even better!

Makes 3 giant cookies

What you'll need:

Cookies:
- 170g caster sugar
- 85g soft dark brown sugar
- 110g butter
- 200g self raising flour
- ½ tsp salt
- 1 large egg
- 100g chocolate chips

Decoration:
- 600g ready-made butter icing
- pony themes decorations
- ready-roll coloured icing and writing icing pens (if you want to decorate the centre of your cookie)

Equipment:
- sieve
- weighing scales
- large mixing bowl
- wooden spoon
- pan (to melt the butter)
- three baking trays, greased and lined with baking parchment
- piping bag and nozzle
- rolling pin

Making the cookies

1 Preheat the oven to 180°C/350°F. Melt the butter in a pan, then leave to cool.

2 Place the caster and brown sugar into a large mixing bowl and stir in the cooled melted butter with a wooden spoon.

3 Beat in the egg and then gently stir in the sifted flour and salt. Carefully mix in the chocolate chips.

4 Divide the dough into three equal pieces of around 230g and place each piece onto a baking tray.

5 Flatten each ball of cookie dough out with the palm of your hand. Bake the cookies for 10-14 minutes or until a golden-brown colour. Leave to cool.

> When the cookies have completely cooled, it's time to decorate them. If you're going to write a message in the centre of your cookies, it's best to do this first

For the centres

1 Dust a work surface with a little icing sugar, then use your rolling pin to flatten out the sugar paste until it's flat and thin. Carefully cut out three circles – you could use an upside-down mug as a guide.

2 Lay each icing circle onto the centre of a cookie and give it a couple of (gentle) goes over with the rolling pin to stick it down.

3 Use the writing icing to create your message – you could pipe your fave pony's name or even a positive saying to boost your confidence!

" Why not make this for a friend, and ice the reason they deserve a rosette?

For the outside

1 Place your piping nozzle into the icing bag. I chose an open star nozzle for mine. Then half-fill the bag with the butter icing in a colour of your choice.

2 Point the nozzle straight down towards the cookie with one hand and gently squeeze the icing bag with the other. As you stop squeezing, push the nozzle slightly down before lifting it up and away to start your next swirl. Continue the whole way around the outside of your cookie.

3 You can make them look even cuter by scattering stars, flowers, horseshoes and other decorations on your cookies.

Oh my gosh! They are so delicious

TACK ATTACK

Your saddle and bridle will look AMAZING with my five-step tack cleaning guide!

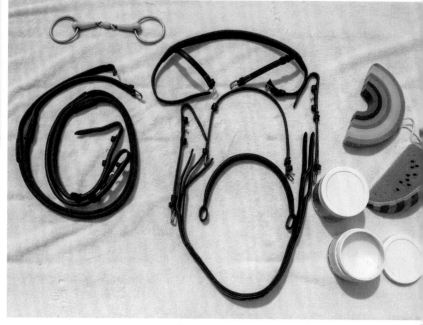

You'll need...

- A bucket of warm water
- Two sponges
- Saddle soap or leather conditioner

1 ☒ Take your bridle apart, and remove the stirrups, leathers and girth from your saddle.

2 ☒ Pop your bit in a bucket of water and give it a good scrub, then wash your stirrup irons.

3 ☒ With clean water, use one of the sponges to wipe over each part of your bridle, saddle and stirrup leathers until they're totally grease-free.

4 ☒ Once they're dry, dampen the other sponge with some fresh water to rub in your saddle soap or use a conditioner. Avoid using too much, or the soap will leave streak marks on your tack.

5 ☒ Once everything's dry, put your bridle back together, and attach your stirrups and leathers to your saddle.

BONDING WITH A
new horse

Finding the right horse was so important to me, but I also really wanted to give Joey the best possible start in his new home

Home sweet home

Joey was born on the farm where we bought him from, so had only known one home. We were worried about how he'd react to a new environment so we tried really hard to get to know his routines, his likes and dislikes and anything that was important to him by talking to his previous owner.

Joey's quite playful, so we got some stable toys to go in his box for when he arrived. He's also very sociable and loves being next door to Mickey – they can almost touch noses if Joey really stretches over the door!

Routine is key

Horses love routine and Joey's no exception. For the first month, we tried to do everything just as it would have been done on the farm, before slowly adjusting things so that Joey could spend more time with Mickey and Casper.

Some people suggest you don't ride a new horse until he's had time to settle in, as horse's behaviour can change when important factors like the amount and quality of sleep they're getting is affected by a move. Others think it's best to continue with the routine a horse is in – especially when they're really fit and might be a bit excited after a break. I talked to his breeder and decided it was best to keep Joey in ridden work, under the guidance of my instructor, and it really seemed to work for him – he's been sooo good!

Keeping things the same on the inside is just as important as external factors, so we concentrated on keeping Joey's diet the same as it was before. I wrote down everything Joey ate, from his hard feed to the amount of hay he gets, and even found out how much he normally drinks so I could quickly tell if he was behaving out of character.

> *Joey was so noisy playing with his toys, he was keeping us awake at night!*

Giving Joey time

I had to tread a careful balance between spending time with Joey to get to know him, and making sure Mickey and Casper still felt loved. They've had all of my attention for such a long time, I knew it might be difficult for them to adapt, too. I chose times when the boys were out in the field together to spend some quality time with Joey – grazing him in hand, finding out where his favourite itchy spots are and generally getting used to his personality.

MAY & JUNE

Summer's coming – and brings with it an endless array of competitions to watch and goals to smash with your fave pony!

The jewel in May's crown is Badminton Horse Trials, which takes place from May 5–9 in 2021. If you love eventing, you won't want to miss it – it's the biggest and best competition in the world, chock full of top riders and horses aiming to impress selectors ahead of the Olympics.

Want to make sure you're ready for show season with your pony? Why not host a series of fun challenges at your yard – who can do the best or fastest plaits, or who can create the neatest quarter marks? You'll have a great laugh while improving your skills ready for the big day!

There are only seven CCI5* events in the world, and the third one takes place from June 17–20. Luhmühlen is tucked away in the north of Germany, about an hour from Hamburg, and it's the ideal summer hol for eventing fans who want to go abroad.

The days are getting longer, which means that hacks with your fave pony can too! If you've got transport, plan some adventures to fill your summer – there are loads of incredible bridleway systems to explore. If your pony can't be ridden, you could even take them for a walk in-hand.

The Global Champions Tour is in full swing by the time May rolls around, so if you love showjumping – and daydreaming about travelling around the world – you'll be spoilt for choice. My dream trip? Madrid in mid-May and Cascais at the end of June. Get your tapas ready!

There's nothing quite like the Hickstead Derby Meeting, which runs at the end of June. Hickstead is Britain's most iconic showjumping venue, and the Derby – which features the famous bank, super-tricky Devil's Dyke and some seriously colossal fences – has to be seen to be believed.

Having fun with Mickey

"When the days get longer, I use the extra daylight hours to spend quality time with all the horses"

On the road

Take a tour around my horsebox and check out my travelling must-haves!

Our little lorry means the horses and I always travel in style when we go out. It's not the biggest, but it has loads of space, and Casper and Joey LOVE travelling in it. So, let's take a tour!

Lights, camera, action!

I always help my Dad check the lights before we go anywhere. This is super-important so other road users can see where we're going!

The cab

This is where Dad and I sit – and where we stash the road trip snacks! There are three seats so if Mum comes with us there's room for everyone. It's super-cool being so close to the horses while we travel – I can even hear Casper munching his hay!

Travel in style

The horses get the best spot in the house when we travel. There's room for two, although we usually only take one, and the partitions are super-easy to move.

There's plenty of space to tie up their haynets and even Joey has enough room to feel comfortable while he travels. The ramp opens in two parts and I love opening the top so Casper can see where we are before he gets off the lorry! The ramp isn't too steep, which makes it nice and easy for the horses to load and unload, too.

The groom's area

There's an awesome storage section at the rear of the lorry, which you can get into through the jockey door or the back of the lorry. It's got little benches so I can chill out, and space to get changed and store all the tack and equipment I need for an outing.

Keeping everything neat

My kit list

Here are some important things I always keep in the lorry ready for an outing...

- spare haynet so that we never run out – even if we get stuck in traffic
- a full show grooming kit – that way I always have everything I need and don't have to worry about forgetting things!
- fresh water and two buckets. One is for the horses to drink out of, and the other's for washing off
- I always have plenty of treats in the lorry to keep the boys happy!
- a spare headcollar and leadrope just in case

45

FUN
FLATWORK

Here are some of my fave flatwork exercises to spice up your schooling sessions!

Super spirals

Handy to help improve your fave pony's bend and balance, spirals are an awesome exercise to try in your next ride.

1. Start in walk on a 20m circle anywhere in the arena and slowly start to make your circle smaller, using your outside aids to do so.
2. Your pony should be looking slightly to the inside, so make sure you're turning your head and shoulders, too.
3. When you get down to a 10m circle, use your inside leg to slowly push your pony back out – he should keep looking to the inside, so try not to use your outside rein.
4. If you and your pony feel confident in walk, have a go in trot and canter – don't make your circle too small though!

Handy to help improve bend and balance, spirals are an awesome exercise!

Listen up!

Top transitions

With a little practise, your fave pony should be listening so carefully you'll be able to push him on and bring him back with barely any effort at all!

1. Start off by trotting around the outside of the arena. Down each long side, push the trot on.
2. On the short sides, see if you can slow him down without letting him walk, slowing the speed of your rising rather than pulling your reins.
3. Next, you can add 15m circles in each corner to help you slow your pony down without having to use super-obvious aids.
4. When you're feeling confident, why not try it in canter? »

Rein it in!

There's nothing better than a stroll on a long rein with your fave pony! Why not practise in the school?

1. Start off in walk with a long rein. Practise steering with your legs and upper body – see how well your pony listens to you.
2. Have a go at stopping him without your reins – it's easier than you think! Sit deep and still in the saddle, lean back a little and use your voice.
3. When you feel totally confident in walk, why not have a go at steering in trot? Your reins are still there if you need them!

Eight is the magic number!

Figure-of-eights are an amazing test of all the things you've tried so far!

1. Get a feel for the figure-of-eight shape in walk. Take care to meet the edge of the arena before you turn down the diagonal.
2. Add a transition at X – what about a walk-halt-walk?
3. Have a go in trot, including transitions at X, either trot-walk-trot or trot-halt-trot.
4. The ultimate test – canter! Make sure you leave plenty of time to change canter lead with a trot transition over X.

This Esme

STUNNING
STABLES

Need some tips to keep your fave pony's stable looking its best? Here are my mucking out hacks!

1. Use your broom to pull down any old cobwebs from the walls and ceiling – there's nothing worse than walking into one of those! Dust collects in old cobwebs, which isn't good for your pony's respiratory system. However, a few active cobwebs will help trap flies in the summer months.

So satisfying!

2. Experiment with the best layout for your pony. If he drops his hay into his water or kicks over his buckets, try keeping them separate or away from the door.

3. Take the time to dig up the banks to stop dirty bedding building up at the bottom of his bed. The more often you do it, the less time it'll take!

4. Tie a scrubbing brush to your tap so there's always one to hand when you need to give your water buckets a scrub – just make sure your pony can't get tangled in it!

5. If you don't have time to muck out the wet every day, try using a layer of soaked wood pellets under your horse's normal bedding. They are super-absorbent and will help to keep bad smells at bay.

6. Stable mats keep your pony super-comfy, but they can get a bit yucky underneath after a while. When you get some free time, pull the rubber mats out of your pony's stable and give them and the floor a thorough clean with disinfectant. It helps get rid of bad smells and will make it much nicer for your pony. Plus it'll make the mats last longer, too!

7. Leave your water buckets under the tap to fill them up while you muck out to save time spent waiting for them to fill afterwards – keep an eye on them so they don't overflow!

Throwback THURSDAYS

Who remembers some of these classic moments?

What's your favourite video of mine?

My first video
Wow, 2015 feels like a really long time ago – I think my editing is much better these days, right?

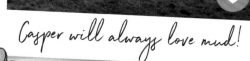

Casper will always love mud!

London Olympia 2015 vlog
The first year I properly vlogged my annual trip to Olympia I was so shy that I didn't even talk to the camera. I absolutely love going and now I get to see all of you at my meet-ups!

Access all areas
You guys love a tack room tour and this video was my initial attempt. It was the first peek at my saddle pad collection and WOW, it's definitely grown since!

So many great surprises!

Mail time
Can you believe Mickey first opened the post way back in 2018? It was really fun doing this series and if you want to go back and watch them head over to my channel.

PONY Photoshoot

Our first ever photoshoot was a lot of fun and we've done so many more since! It's always super-cool seeing how the photos turn out and being able to look back on the day. I never thought I would have a shoot for my own yearbook!

My saddle pad collection

This was one of the most requested videos. It was so fun showing you all the amazing colours in my collection.

Riding at Hickstead

Without YouTube this video never would've happened. I still feel so lucky to have had the opportunity of riding in the international arena – and up and down the Hickstead bank.

My ever-growing collection!

Travelling around Australia

Going down under in 2019 was incredible. I got to see so many amazing animals, cuddle a koala, visit a 5* eventer and vlog the Australian three-day event in Adelaide – phew! If you haven't watched them, grab a cup of hot chocolate, make yourself comfy on the sofa and enjoy!

Helping in Senegal with the Brooke

This was one of the most rewarding videos I have ever made. Working with Brooke in Senegal was a massive life experience for me. Being able to help both people and animals makes my YouTube job so rewarding.

Who wants a cuddle?

2010 vs 2020

It wouldn't be a #ThrowbackThursday without a little mention of my ten years with Mickey video!

BARN TOUR

Come behind the stable door for a special look at what's new for Willow, Bruno and Toby

Most of you know the donkeys are like family to me. They've all lived on the farm since before I was born, and last winter we decided it was time we treated them to a new barn. Let me give you a tour of their new home!

TIP TOP TOES

Donkeys originate from countries with hot climates and dry, stony ground. Their hooves can't tolerate the wet ground that often comes with our rainy winters in the UK, because they've evolved to absorb water much more efficiently than horses' hooves. This means their feet can become soft and suffer from hoof problems.

When we built the new barn, we also created a large area of hard standing so that the donkeys have a place that's mud-free to hang out – no matter what the weather.

This was the donkeys' old home

Willow

Bruno

Toby

The skylights make it light and airy

KNOCK KNOCK

Donkeys are much smaller than horses and most ponies, so they need smaller doors. It sounds obvious, but it's actually quite difficult to find the perfect size door that keeps them safe while allowing them to look out. These doors, which should be the top door for a horse, worked perfectly for Willow, Bruno and Toby.
For most of the year our donkeys are free to roam in and out of their barn, but when the weather is extreme, or one of them is unwell, we need to be able to bring them in for their own benefit. »

> **The new barn is the perfect place for Toby, Bruno and Willow**

DONKEY DIETS

It's easy for donkeys to become overweight in the UK where the grass is luscious, so we have to keep an eye on their waistlines at all times. Bruno's definitely the greediest donkey we have! To keep them in top condition we restrict their grazing area and only give them very small quantities of fibre-based feed that's suitable for donkeys.

They say sharing is caring!

MATCHY-MATCHY

Willow, Bruno and Toby were also treated to these gorgeous matching fly rugs. They keep the flies off and stop the donkeys from rubbing on fences and trees in their paddock. We call them their matching PJs because they look so cute! Unfortunately not everyone loved the donkeys new look as much as I do – both Joey and Casper spooked at them the first time they saw their new outfits!

Did you know?

Donkey's coats don't have a natural build up of grease like horses do, so their coats aren't waterproof. This makes it especially important for them to have a dry field shelter or stable, so they can avoid the elements.

The donkeys' matching name plaques

Willow

Bruno

Toby

BFFs

Donkeys form pair bonds and should never be separated from their special friend. Toby and Bruno have the closest bond of our three donkeys, but they all get on so well.

When we built the new barn it was important that there was plenty of room for all of them. Unlike horses, donkeys don't like to have individual stables – they much prefer to share.

JULY & AUGUST

There's nothing better than endless days at the stables when it sizzles – no school, no worries – just ponies, ponies, ponies. Bliss!

Keep cool in the heat by stocking the yard freezer with ice lollies – for people and ponies! You can make a delicious pony-friendly popsicle by filling a small feed bucket with cold water and slices of apple and carrot. Freeze and then serve to your pony just like a lick – and don't forget to treat yourself to a Solero for your hard work!

Don't miss Concours Hippique International Officiel (CHIO) Aachen from June 29 – July 4. It hosts top-level showjumping, dressage, eventing, vaulting, and carriage-driving all in one unbelievable venue. My recommendation? Don't miss the Ride and Drive that teams up eventers, jumpers and drivers in a crazy relay race.

The Royal International Horse Show at Hickstead hosts a Nations Cup team event, which means that you can see some of the best riders from around the world in Sussex. Don't miss the Eventers' Grand Prix on Thursday to see famous faces tackle the challenge of the international arena, too!

The Tokyo Olympics will be the highlight of the summer, and while you might not be able to hop on a plane to Japan, you'll still be able to follow every bit of the action. This year's competition sees new rules across many of the disciplines and is sure to be an event you won't want to miss!

Don't miss the Nations Cup!

Mad about pony novels? Start a book club with your friends. Take it in turns to pick a horsey book and then get together to chat about it after you've finished. It's a great way to connect with your social media pals, too – you could even host your meetings on Zoom.

The Global Champions Tour makes its way to London in August. Join showjumping's brightest stars at the Royal Hospital, Chelsea, for a glamorous showcase of sport in the city!

> Summer can be a whirlwind of competitions and events, but it's important to give your pony a break, too

This Esme

Yeeha!

I've always wanted to try Western riding and last year I got the chance to put on my cowboy boots and give it a go!

What to wear

Traditionally Western riders wear jeans, cowboy boots and Stetsons – but I'll be sticking to my safety helmet.

TALKING TACK

Western saddles are quite different to English tack. They are heavier and you can't run the stirrups up in the same way – you have to throw the saddle up in the air so that the stirrups clear the horse's back, before gently lowering it into place. The shape is also different to support a longer leg position for the rider's comfort, because cowboys would often be in the saddle all day. The most obvious distinction is the pommel – it's much bigger and has a horn on the top that's used as a place to hang lassos and other equipment.

Western saddles have two girths, the cinch, which is the main girth, and a flank strap, which has a looser fit and is designed to keep the saddle in place when you're riding downhill. Most Western saddles also feature incredibly beautiful designs and patterns within the leatherwork.

Some Western bridles have an earpiece, which encircles one of the horses' ears, instead of a headpiece. You also have special reins called split reins which aren't buckled together like English reins. There's usually no noseband, unless the bridle is bitless, and a rope halter is sometimes left on underneath the bridle.

Did you know?
Western riding evolved from cattle ranching.

Did you know?
The most popular horses used for Western riding are Quarter Horses who got their name for being the fastest breed to gallop over a quarter of a mile. Paints, Appaloosas, Arabs, Saddlebreds and Morgans are also popular horses for Western riding. »

REIN IT IN

Western riding evolved with the reins being held in one hand in an upright fist so that the cowboys had one hand free to manage their cattle, open and close gates or lead spare horses. Traditionally the reins are held in the left hand, leaving the right free for these tasks. If the reins are joined, they're held with the reins coming up through the bottom of your fist, through the palm, and out the top of your hand. However, if you're riding with split reins they go from the top of your fist, out the bottom and then hang down the horse's shoulder. Western horses are ridden with a very light hand – you don't have a contact with the bit, instead the rein is loose. When you want to turn you move your hand so that the rein crosses the horse's neck indicating which way to go.

It felt strange to ride with no rein contact!

Getting to grips with Western tack

LOPING ALONG

There isn't much trotting in Western riding, because everything is done sitting in the saddle without rising. Instead, Western riders tend to walk or gallop – or as they call it, lope. It's incredibly exhilarating to be loping through the vast and dramatic landscapes of the USA and it's surprisingly comfortable, too!

Did you know?
Stables in the USA are known as ranches, where cowboys traditionally look after cattle as well as horses.

"It's incredibly exhilarating to be loping through the vast and dramatic landscapes of the USA, and surprisingly comfortable, too!"

Make a horseshoe dream catcher

Make sure every night's filled with awesome pony-filled dreams by making this super-cool dream catcher

let's get started

What you'll need:
- a horseshoe – ideally with stud holes
- 1m length of string
- decorations of your choice

1

Clean your horseshoe thoroughly to get rid of any mud, and make sure it's completely dry. Take one end of your string and tie it securely through one of the stud holes.

Top tip
Make an extra couple of loops on the string which goes across the top of the horseshoe, to keep the weaving pattern circular.

2

Thread your string through the first nail hole, and pass it back through the loop you've just made – like a blanket stitch. Pull it tight before continuing around the horseshoe until you're back to the start – going straight across at the top.

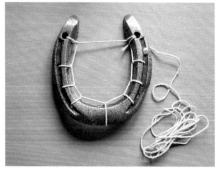

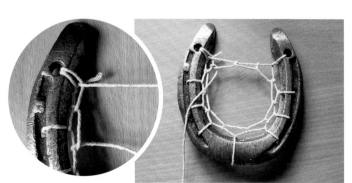

3

Continue threading and looping your string, but instead of using the nail holes, pass the string through the loops you created in step 2.

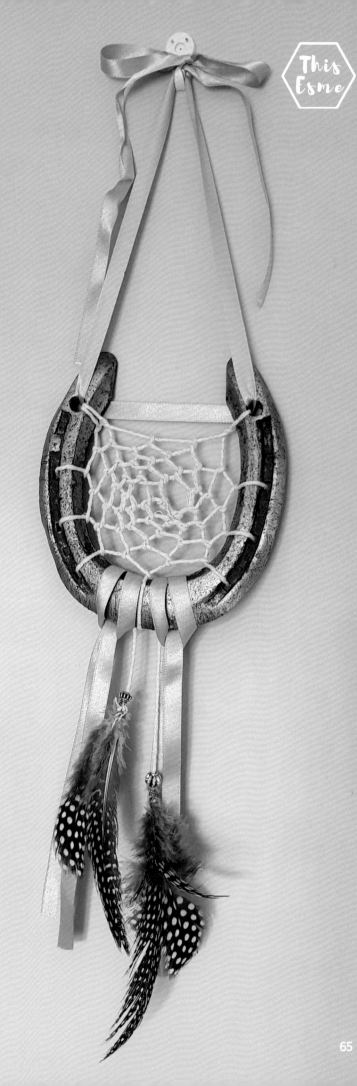

4 Keep going until your pattern fills the centre of the shoe. Then, tie the string to itself and cut off any excess.

5 Decorate your dream catcher and add some ribbon to hang it up by. I've finished mine with feathers and ribbon, but you could thread beads on, too.

Try experimenting with different types of string and you could even paint your horseshoe first!

Top tip

Attach feathers to lengths of string by wrapping wire around the two. Carefully tuck in the ends so they aren't sharp.

HICKSTEAD

HICKSTEAD

HICKSTEAD

YouTube has given me some of the most amazing experiences that would never have been possible without it

CASPER'S
glow up

Here's my guide to getting Casper competition-ready with top tips to help you prepare for a show day!

Grey saddle pad

Saddle and stud girth

Tendon and fetlock boots for jumping

Riding hat

Bridle

Gloves

Show shirt and jacket

White breeches

We love getting glammed up in our show gear

Long boots

Other items to remember...
- stock
- bridle number for dressage
- long or short whip
- fly bonnet »

Before a competition day I make sure to get every job ticked off with plenty of time to spare...

- clean tack and riding boots
- get Casper's travel boots, tail bandage and guard ready
- pack water with two buckets
- check my spare grooming kit, headcollar and leadrope are in the lorry
- fill two haynets
- write down my competition times and leave them in the lorry so I don't forget
- put copies of my dressage tests in the lorry in case I can't remember them
- double check that my competition outfit is clean and ready to go
- bath Casper and plait him up the night before so I only have to give him a quick spruce up in the morning!

Don't forget to pack your pony's haynet for the journey!

Did you know?

Ponies' digestive systems need a steady stream of fibre, like hay or chaff, to work best. Make sure your pony has plenty of hay to munch on at the show. You could even pack a small chaff feed to keep his tummy happy!

A tail guard and travel boots are essential protective gear

HACKING WITH JOEY

Casper and I have ridden here, there and everywhere together, but when Joey arrived, we got to explore everything all over again!

Two's company

I'm very lucky to have some amazing horsey friends right on the doorstep who have been really helpful in accompanying me and Joey on our early hacks. As horses are herd animals, they get a lot of comfort from being with other horses, so it was important that we found Joey some hacking buddies to help him feel confident in his new surroundings. Even though Joey's young, he has a very laid-back attitude to hacking and seems to really enjoy it.

Heading out

I like to start all my hacks with a 5-10 minute walk. It gives the horses time to warm up their muscles and it gives me the opportunity to assess how they're feeling. It's really important with a young horse like Joey that I always ask him to walk forward positively and make sure that he's listening to my aids. That way, if he looks at something, I can reassure him and ask him to continue past whatever is causing him to spook. I like to stroke his neck with my hand and praise him with my voice, so he knows he's been good.

Safety first

It's a good idea to wear high-vis whenever you're hacking, even if you aren't going on any roads. Making yourself visible gives other bridlepath users like cyclists and runners the opportunity to slow down, making it much safer for everyone. High-vis also makes it easier for emergency services to find you, should the worst happen and you part company with your horse.

Top tip

Try to avoid cantering in the same places every time you hack out. If you do, you may quickly find that your pony anticipates a good canter and gets a bit silly.

Desensitisation

I do a lot of filming work with the horses, but it doesn't happen overnight. Before we go somewhere exciting to shoot a video – like the beach – I make sure the horses are 100% comfortable being around all the equipment, which can involve drones or even my dad on his bike alongside us. We practise all of this in the fields at home, which the horses know and feel safe in, so that they aren't worried. Very quickly our various gadgets become part of their daily lives and now they don't bat an eyelid!

Riding out is one of the greatest things about owning horses

Spice it up

One of the main reasons I love hacking so much is that it really breaks up the horses' training and it's great for keeping them fit. I like to do lots of trot work and use this time to get rid of any excess energy they have before we have a canter. Going up and down hills is so good for them and will play a big part in helping to strengthen Joey's muscles as he grows and develops.

There are days when I want hacking to be all about fun – for me and the horses – but there are other times when I use the great outdoors as my training ground and ride lots of transitions, and even practise my lateral work!

SEPTEMBER & OCTOBER

School's in session – but that doesn't mean that ponies need to take a back seat!

Autumn doesn't begin until the Land Rover Burghley Horse Trials kicks off at the beginning of September. Burghley's known for being the biggest of all the CCI5* events – and once you've walked the course and seen the Cottesmore Leap with its huge SUV-sized ditch, you'll understand why!

For ages, Kentucky in April has been the USA's only five-star event, but new kid on the block is October fixture Fair Hill. With a meaty course designed by eventing legend Ian Stark and stars like Boyd Martin and Phillip Dutton on the roster, it's an action-packed way to start the month.

Want to compete, but not quite ready this year? Get your fix by signing up as a volunteer at an autumn one-day event or hunter trial. Bring your best friend and sign up as fence judges or ring stewards – you'll enjoy a pony-packed day, lots of good food, and you might even be given a schooling voucher as thanks!

Want to incorporate your love of ponies into your schoolwork? Easy peasy. Why not write a book report on National Velvet by Enid Bagnold, research equine cloning for a science paper or dive into the curious story of war horse Sergeant Reckless for history?

The FEI Nations Cup showjumping series comes to an exciting conclusion in Barcelona. Sunshine, enormous fences, famous riders and the final fight for glory – you'll be hooked!

Catch me at Burghley

The European eventing season comes to a close at Les Etoiles de Pau, France's only CCI5* event. Nestled in the foothills of the Pyrennees by the border to Spain, this sunny, friendly event features a twisty, tricky course and the best food you'll ever find at a horse show – truffles anyone?

"As the nights draw in, take time out to enjoy the occasional warm sunset"

INSIDE MY
grooming kit

Find out what essentials I have in my grooming kit to keep my equines looking their absolute best!

Hoof pick
Use before and after every ride, plus when your pony comes in or out, to keep his feet healthy.

Hoof dressing
Not just to make him look smart, some hoof oils can also strengthen hooves and help them grow.

Metal or plastic curry comb
Use this one to clean your body brush so you don't brush dirt back onto your pony!

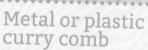

Conditioner

This keeps your pony's coat shiny and his mane and tail super sleek and easy to comb. Be careful if you do use it on his mane, though – it can make your reins slippy!

Rubber curry comb

An awesome shedding tool, rubber curry combs can also help get rid of dirt in your pony's coat.

Mane/tail brush

A gentle comb to get through your pony's mane and tail.

Magic brush

This is for super-stubborn mud or stains in your pony's coat!

Body brush

For stable-kept ponies to get rid of dust and grease in their coats.

Sponges

Separate ones for his eyes, nose, dock and body!

Soft face brush

If your pony's sensitive you could use this instead of the body brush to keep his face clean.

Dandy brush

Use this on your pony's body if he's unclipped and lives out. Avoid sensitive areas though.

OVER
WE GO

Have a go at my fave polework exercises to make your schooling sesh super-fun!

> Keep your pony super-straight. He might wobble as the poles look a bit different to usual

E

EXERCISE 1
Diamonds are forever

This layout builds from the classic box, which is one of my all-time favourites, and it's a great way to spice up your usual polework routines!

1. Set up two diamonds using eight poles with their ends touching.
2. Walk and trot through the diamonds on both reins. I like to ride down the middle, but there are so many routes you can try.
3. Make sure to keep your pony super-straight. He might wobble as the poles look a bit different to usual.
4. Try a downward transition in the middle of the first diamond, and an upward transition in second one.
5. If you're feeling confident try cantering down the line of poles – you could even ride a canter-trot transition in the first diamond and trot-canter in the second. »

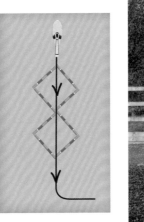

Get creative by using the sides of the diamonds as well as the corners

EXERCISE 2
Super serpentines

How good are your serpentines? Let's make them perfect with this cool layout!

1. Set out two poles along the centre line. The centre of the top and bottom poles should sit in the middle of B and F and B and M.
2. Complete your serpentine in walk first, riding straight over the middle of each pole as you ask your pony to change his bend.
3. Try it in trot, riding smooth turns and changing diagonal as you go over each pole.
4. If you're ready, try a transition over each pole, like trot-walk-trot or even canter-trot-canter with a lead change if you're feeling brave!

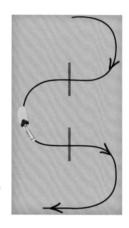

Look to your next pole as you turn off the track

Top tip

Polework is really hard work for your pony, so don't try all the exercises on the same day!

EXERCISE 3
Wonky lines

Keep your pony on the straight and narrow with this cool exercise.

1. Set up four to six poles at angles with 2.7m between the centre of each one.
2. Walk and trot in a straight line through the poles, making sure you ride over the middle of each one.
3. Try trotting through the poles slightly to the left or right of the centre to test how accurately you can ride the line – does your pony run out or drift back to the middle?
4. Have a go in canter! Make sure you keep him straight and your shoulders up to avoid unbalancing him.

Top tip

Raised poles will make your fave pony work extra hard, so make plenty of changes of rein and give him lots of breaks.

EXERCISE 4
Enter the maze

This is an awesome layout to help you learn to bend and straighten your pony super-smoothly.

1. Set out your maze using six poles, leaving a 1.3m-wide path for you to ride through.
2. Have a go at walking through the poles, carefully bending your pony's body around each turn. Remember, your legs are just as important for steering your pony as your hands!
3. Have a trot over the poles that line up – the 1.3m distance should be perfect.
4. Focus on straightness by trotting into the maze from one side, through a channel of poles and changing the rein as you ride out the other side.

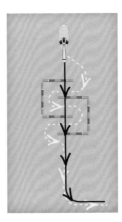

Trotting through the pole channels is great for working on straightness

Look straight ahead as you trot through the poles

A DAY IN THE LIFE

Lots has changed since I finished my A levels.
School's out, but I seem to be busier than ever!

6AM

It's breakfast time – but not for me! I pull on some clothes and head out onto the yard to give the horses and donkeys their breakfast. Once I've given them all a feed, I head to the chicken coop to let the hens out into their run, give them some breakfast and check for any eggs. Then it's time for me to head into the house for something to eat myself. I check my messages and respond to as many as I can while munching some toast.

7AM

Time to head back onto the yard and let the horses out into their field. I've got a lesson later today, so I want the horses to enjoy as much time as possible in their paddock beforehand. I skip out all the stables and fill a fresh bucket of water for Casper – who still doesn't like sharing!

8AM

Time for me to go for a quick run. I'm so lucky to have plenty of paths to choose from literally on the doorstep, so I put my trainers on and waste no time.

8.30AM

There's just enough time for a quick shower before I start work.

9AM

I've got a heap of video editing to do from the footage we shot at the weekend, so I settle at my desk for what will be a solid morning's work. Everyone needs the odd screen break from time to time and I spend mine looking out of the window to see if the horses are doing anything interesting that I can catch on my phone. Today it seems they're very content eating grass.

12NOON

I'm sooo ready for lunch! Today I'm having vegetable quiche and salad. After eating I can't resist a spot of Animal Crossing on the sofa!

1PM

Dad's got a free afternoon and has agreed to help me film a new intro for the video I'm editing this week. I get all the clothes I'll need for the shoot ready and take them to the yard.

2PM

I head back onto the yard, bring the horses in from the field and make sure everything's ready for filming. I'm so lucky my dad's a keen videographer and is as passionate about my channel as I am. We film a few segments and it's all wrapped up within the hour.

3PM

It's time to get ready for my lesson at 3.30. I've already got my breeches on, so it doesn't take long. I've got a few minutes to spare so I have a quick selfie sesh with Joey, who almost eats my phone in the process.

3.30PM

Today I've got back-to-back lessons with Joey and Casper. First, we're concentrating on poles to improve Joey's straightness and my steering.

4.15PM

My instructor gives me a hand untacking Joey while I quickly tack up Casper, then we head back to the arena. I've been working really hard on impulsion with Casper and it's starting to pay off. I'm thrilled with both the boys today and there'll definitely be extra carrots in their dinners!

5PM

It's time to finish the chores for the horses. Making haynets, evening feeds and breakfasts for the morning – not to mention filling water buckets for everyone. I put Joey, Casper and Mickey to bed and give the donkeys their evening feeds. Then I pop back to the house for a quick snack for myself.

6PM

I'm back out on the yard – but this time I'm concentrating on getting everything ready for a big shoot we have planned for the following day. I harrow the school so that it looks amazing. When I'm done, I spot that Casper is pulling the cutest sleepy face so I take a quick film for my TikTok and I'm already thinking about what soundtrack to put with it.

7PM

Feeling pretty exhausted I head back to the house and get changed before joining my family for dinner.

8PM

I give the horses their final check for the evening and pop the hens in their coop for the night.

8.30PM

I chill-out on the sofa watching a bit of YouTube and WhatsApp my friends.

At home or away, I'm always super-busy!

ICELANDIC ADVENTURES

Last year I travelled to Iceland to meet and ride the iconic Icelandic horses. Enjoy an insight into what it's really like to ride these amazing little horses

THE ORIGINS OF THE SPECIES

The first Viking settlers brought horses to Iceland a thousand years ago, and for more than 800 years they haven't been mixed with other breeds. As a result, Icelandic horses are considered one of the purest breeds in the world. They've evolved to cope with the harsh, rugged conditions of Iceland, which is just south of the Arctic Circle. This has made them strong, sure-footed and famed for their stamina and endurance.

The horses of Iceland have been so cut-off from other equine populations that they don't have any resistance to common horse diseases found across Europe and the United States. As a result, once a horse leaves Iceland it can never return – this protects the horses living in Iceland from exposure to infection. Visitors to the island have to thoroughly disinfect their riding gear before travelling to Iceland for the same reason.

Did you know?
In summer the sun only sets for around three hours a day, so it's effectively light 24/7.

VITAL STATS

Height: 13-14hh
Colour: chestnut, dun, bay, black, grey, palomino, pinto and roan to name a few. There are more than 100 names for their various coat colours in the Icelandic language
Weight: 330-380kg ⟫

GOING THROUGH THE GEARS

Icelandic horses have the same basic paces as other horses – they can walk trot, canter and gallop – but they also have something that sets them apart from other breeds. They have a unique pace called the tölt. This is a four-beat gait and shares the same footfalls as walk – left hind, left front, right hind, then right front, however it can be performed at all speeds, from that of a fast walking pace right up to a canter. It's really comfortable for the rider as there's no moment of suspension – one of the horse's feet is always on the ground.

Some Icelandic horses are referred to as five-gaited horses, this means they can walk, trot, canter and gallop, tölt and pace. Often called the flying pace, it's a two-beat gait where the front and hindlegs on the same side move together in pairs. This is mostly used for racing and some horses can achieve speeds of up to 30mph!

Did you know?
Icelandic horses are all referred to as horses, even though they're only the height of a pony.

Did you know?
In Iceland you don't pat horses, you only ever stroke them.

The new match-matchy

There's an Icelandic saying that translates as "A good horse has no colour"– it means you should see past the horse's coat. There are so many colour variations of Icelandic horse, it's one of the things that attracts people to the breed. Literally any colour – apart from spotted – is allowed by the breed standard, from exotic looking silver dapple blue roans to piebald and cremellos to black horses – there really is a whole rainbow of coat colours to choose from!

TRADITIONAL TACK

Icelandic saddles are slightly different to those used for English riding. Not dissimilar to a dressage saddle, they have long saddle flaps with a large knee roll at the front – but the seat is shallower. In Icelandic riding, riders don't rise to the trot and the tölt is also ridden seated, so the saddle reflects this – making it comfortable for riders to spend all day riding. You'll notice a difference in the stirrups, too, as they hang facing forward so the leather lays flat against the saddle, reducing the risk of rubs for the rider.

Such ornate stirrup irons!

"A good horse has no colour"

Make a lantern

#CASPERFRIENDLYGHOSTHORSE

You all know Casper's hashtag, so why not have a go at carving your very own Casper pumpkin?

let's get started

What you'll need:
- a pumpkin, turnip or squash
- scissors
- sticky tape
- template on page 101
- spoon
- cocktail stick or skewer
- sharp knife

1

Using the sharp knife, cut around the stalk in a circle – this needs to be large enough for you to be able to get your hand inside your pumpkin later. Then pull the stalk so that the top comes completely off.

Top tip

You can save the inside of the pumpkin and the seeds to cook later.

2

Using your spoon, hollow out your pumpkin. Make sure you remove all the seeds and soft inner flesh.

3

Cut out the template on page 101 or trace it onto a piece of paper and stick it to the side of your pumpkin using sticky tape.

4

Using a cocktail stick or skewer, pierce a dotted line around your template. Make sure you go through the paper and the skin of the pumpkin.

Top tip
The muck heap is the perfect place to grow your own pumpkin for next year!

5

Remove your template, then very carefully cut along the dotted outline to create your Casper-shaped hole in the side of your pumpkin.

Place a nightlight inside your pumpkin and display it in the window!

Trick or treat?

> *Casper would choose a treat every time!*

NOVEMBER & DECEMBER

Does your Christmas list start and end with one request – a pony of your own? Here are my tips for embracing the winter months

☑ Once the competition season ends, many famous riders start teaching clinics all over the world. Follow your faves on social media or check out their website to see if they'll be hosting one near you – whether you bring your fave pony for a lesson or simply go along to watch, you'll have a fab day and learn loads.

☑ Heading to the city to find horses sounds crazy, right? Wrong! Most major cities have a museum dedicated to the cavalry – London's is at Horseguards, where you'll see regimental horses on duty. Or you can check out famous urban equines such as the Lipizzaners at Vienna's Spanish Riding School or racehorses at Paris' Bois de Boulogne!

☑ The final CCI5* of the year takes place in Adelaide, Australia in November. If you're in denial about the off-season, you won't want to miss it!

My meet-up in Adelaide!

☑ You're guaranteed to get that festive feeling after a visit to Olympia. No matter when you visit, you'll enjoy amazing performances, super showjumping, the best horsey shopping in the world and celeb sightings, but Wednesday night is particularly great – that's when the famous puissance is held, with top riders attempting to scale heights of 2m or more!

☑ Make an edible Christmas garland for your fave pony by stringing apples, carrots and Polo mints onto baling twine and hanging it in his stable. Make it look extra festive by tying sprigs of hay in between the fruit and veg.

☑ Want to ensure a super-horsey start to 2022? End the year at the Liverpool Horse Show, which combines showjumping with live music and BMX stunts for the ultimate New Year's Eve party.

66 I love riding out on cold crisp mornings with Casper 99

CLIPPING
WITH CASPER

Here's how I decide which clip to give Casper, and some of my tips for the perfect clip

WHICH CLIP?

Before I get the clippers out it's important to think about what sort of work I'll be doing with the horses, and whether they'll be living in the field 24-7 or coming into their stables at night. Here are a few of my fave clips and what they're best for:

Before you start

- give your pony a really good groom before you get the clippers out. Mud and dirt clogs the clipper blades and makes them blunt
- make sure your clipper blades are sharp, and have been oiled
- tie a haynet up for your pony to munch on
- if you have a dark coloured pony it's really helpful to mark out the lines of your clip with chalk so that you have a guide

Top tip
Your pony may feel fresh for a few days after you've clipped him, so you may want to lunge before you ride.

Bib clip
This is when the hair is only clipped from the pony's throat, chest and the bottom of his belly. It was great for Mickey when he was semi-retired and I was only riding him 2-3 times a week, because it just removed hair from the areas where he sweated most – leaving him plenty of coat to keep warm.

Neck and belly clip
This clip extends the bib clip so that the hair is removed from his shoulders and more of his belly. It's good for ponies in light work as they still have plenty of coat to keep them warm, but you don't have to worry about them getting too hot and sweaty when you are able to ride them.

Trace clip
This clip follows a line that goes half way down the neck, removing hair from the lower part, then extends along your pony's sides to his quarters. It's a really useful clip as it can be adjusted to sit higher or lower on the horse, depending on what level of work they're doing and how sweaty they get.

Top tip

Run the clippers within earshot of your pony to see how he reacts. If he's nervous, repeat this every day, slowly getting closer to him so that he learns there is nothing to be scared of.

Casper gets so hairy!

The perfect clip

- take your time with the clippers and stay calm – ponies pick up on stress and it makes them worried
- clip against the direction of the hair's growth – the opposite to how you groom
- start low down on your pony's neck to help him settle and so that you can change to a smaller clip if you need to
- finish up by wiping your horse over with a hot cloth to remove any little bits of hair that might be itchy
- make sure you rug your pony appropriately – he'll miss that fur when it's cold

Blanket clip

This time the whole of the neck comes off and a 'blanket' is left on the pony's back, which prevents ponies getting chilly while being ridden on cold mornings. Ponies who have this clip will definitely need to be rugged through the winter and it's ideal for ponies who are ridden 4-6 times a week.

Full clip

This is when all of a pony's coat is clipped apart from a saddle patch. It's normally only used by owners whose ponies are in hard work and are ridden daily. This clip isn't suitable for ponies who live out, and they'll need to have a warm, waterproof winter rug to wear in the field as well as a stable rug.

Next-level
matchy-matchy

You know me – matchy-matchy doesn't stop with saddle pads and base layers. Here's how you can achieve my colour co-ordinated looks

I love to match everything in my equine life, from the things I use everyday around the yard, to the kit I keep in my horsebox. It's even started creeping into my non-horsey life – who knew that my sliders matching my hoodie perfectly would become a priority? Not me... but here I am!

STEP 1: PICK A COLOUR

Start by choosing the colour you'd like to see all around the yard. If you have my yearbook from last year, you could use the colour wheel to find the perfect match for your horse.

STEP 2: PICK WHERE THIS COLOUR IS GOING TO GO

Each of my horses has a set colour for their gear – Mickey's blue, Casper's purple, Joey's green, Willow's pink, Bruno's red and Toby has orange. All their buckets, headcollars and grooming kits match. It keeps everything personal and it's also a great hack for when my Mum has to look after the horses while I'm travelling!

STEP 3: CO-ORDINATE FOR DIFFERENT ASPECTS OF HORSEY LIFE

For me, I like different colours for different occasions. I've kept all my equipment for when we go out in the horsebox grey. It makes everything so organised, and every photo we get while we're out and about looks super-smart. A massive plus is this neutral colour goes perfectly with every horse, too!

I've also tried to keep all of my jumps in the arena co-ordinated in bright colours. I always build the fences with either matching or complimentary coloured poles so they look great in videos.

STEP 4: WHAT IF I CAN'T GET AN ITEM IN MY COLOUR MATCH?

If you're struggling to find equipment in a specific colour, don't panic! When I can't find the exact shade want, I pick a neutral or complimentary colour instead. It's good to go for a grey, navy or black because they tend to blend in with the rest of your kit perfectly – no one will notice, trust me!

STEP 5: DIY!

You don't have to spend loads of money to get everything matching! I'm a really big fan of DIY and it's a great way to get your jumps, bridle hooks, name plates and small details around the yard colour

co-ordinated. I'm really lucky because we keep our horses on our own property, so make sure you have permission from your yard owner before the change anything. A quick and easy DIY tip is to paint your hooks and name plates to match each other – and why not paint a horseshoe like I do?

STEP 6: TAKE SOME PHOTOS

Once you're all matching and co-ordinated, it's time to get some photos for the 'gram – make sure you tag me in your matchy looks! #ThisEsmeMatchy

> **Matchy-matchy looks cute, but it also has a practical element to it**

Casper

ARE YOU A SUPER-FAN?

Have you read your yearbook from cover to cover? Do you know all there is to know about my herd of equines? Take the quiz and test your knowledge!

1 How old was I when I got Mickey? - - - - - - - - - - - - - - - - -

2 What is the name given to a male donkey? - - - - - - - - - - - - - -

3 What breed is Joey? - - - - - - - - - - - - - -

4 How many horses can travel in my horsebox? - - - - - - - - - - - -

5 How many cookies does the rosette recipe make? - - - - - - - - - -

6 When did I first vlog from the Olympia London International horse show? - - - - - - - - - - -

7 What game do I love playing on my phone? - - - - - - - - - - - -

8 What is my TikTok username? - - - - - - - - - - - - -

9 What is galloping known as in Western riding?

10 What colour is my travelling grooming kit?

11 For how long has the Icelandic breed of horses been considered pure?

12 Which amazing 5* event did I visit in Australia?

13 What is Casper's hash tag?

14 Which family member helps by videoing me?

15 What is Willow's colour?

16 What kind of clip does Casper normally have?

17 At which famous international arena was I allowed to ride Casper to the top of a derby bank?

18 With which charity did I travel to Senegal?

19 What is the name of my favourite hen?

Turn to page 100 for the answers!

20 What breed of chicken is Mars?

THE SECRET LANGUAGE OF
HORSES

Want to know what your fave pony's thinking?
Let's find out!

Casper's eyes look relaxed and bright. If your pony is upset or frightened, he might have wrinkles around his eyes.

His ears are always forward, especially when there's food involved! This means he's happy, but if your pony's ears are flat back then stay away! Sometimes Casper's ears flick to the side and back, he does this because he's listening to everything that's going on around him.

If your fave pony swishes his tail a lot – and it's not because he's keeping the flies away – it could be that he's uncomfortable or upset. If he does this regularly make sure you get him checked out by your vet, saddler and physio.

Casper sometimes likes to rest one of his hind legs when he's feeling super-relaxed. If your fave pony does this it just means he's mega chilled, but if he's resting a front leg you should definitely call your vet.

Did you know?
Your fave pony's ears can turn 180 degrees! This means he can listen super-carefully in any direction.

Field friends

It's easy to see how well Mickey and Casper get on with each other because they're comfortable laying down and rolling near one another. Horses feel vulnerable when they aren't standing up, so it's a sign of trust and friendship that Mickey and Casper do this all the time. When the horses are out at night, they normally take turns to watch out for the other while he sleeps. It's all part of being in a herd and ensures everyone is safe.

...reat, just when I'd got them clean...

Is three a crowd?

When Joey joined the heard, I was worried how it would impact the dynamic between Mickey and Casper. Initially I put Joey in the field next to them, so they could all get to know each other while still having the option of their own space. However, it wasn't long before they were grooming each other over the fence and seemed so settled as a group that I was able to turn them out together as one big happy family.

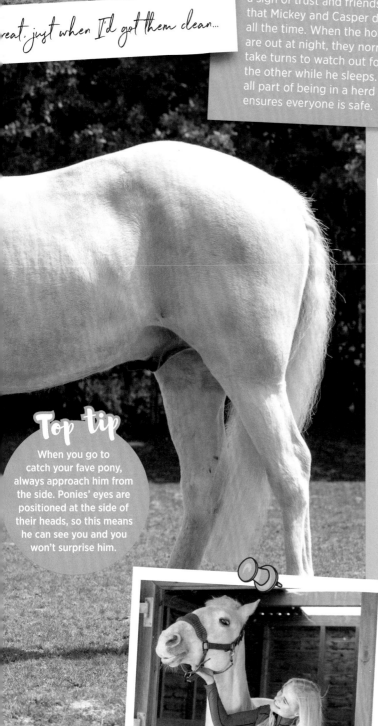

Top tip

When you go to catch your fave pony, always approach him from the side. Ponies' eyes are positioned at the side of their heads, so this means he can see you and you won't surprise him.

What a catch!

I'm sooo lucky that my equines are good to catch, but I know not everyone has it so easy! Here's my quick pony-catching guide...

- spend time chilling out in the field with your pony. Don't take a headcollar, just give him some treats and a pat if he comes over to say hi
- when your pony comes to you every time, take a headcollar and wait for him
- give him a treat and loop the lead rope round his neck before putting on his headcollar. Give him a scratch or treat and remove the headcollar
- do this often and he'll realise he doesn't have to work or come in each time you catch him, which should make him lots happier to be caught!

Ahhh, that's the spot!

Scratchy spots

Mickey and Casper love grooming each other – but did you know ponies enjoy a good scratch from us, too? Why not spend time finding your pony's best itchy spot? His pony pals will give you clues by scratching places he likes, but he might like his chest, withers or forehead being rubbed, too. It's an awesome way to bond with your fave pony and he's sure to love it, too!

Answers and Templates

Find all the answers and things you need here!

PAGE 22
WORDSEARCH

SPOT THE DIFFERENCE

PAGE 96
SUPER-FAN QUIZ

1. Eight
2. Jack
3. Warmblood x Thoroughbred
4. Two
5. Three
6. 2015
7. Animal crossing
8. This_Esme
9. Lope
10. Grey

11. 800 years
12. Adelaide
13. #Casperfriendlyghosthorse
14. My dad
15. Pink
16. Blanket
17. Hickstead
18. Brooke
19. Snickers
20. Rhode Rock

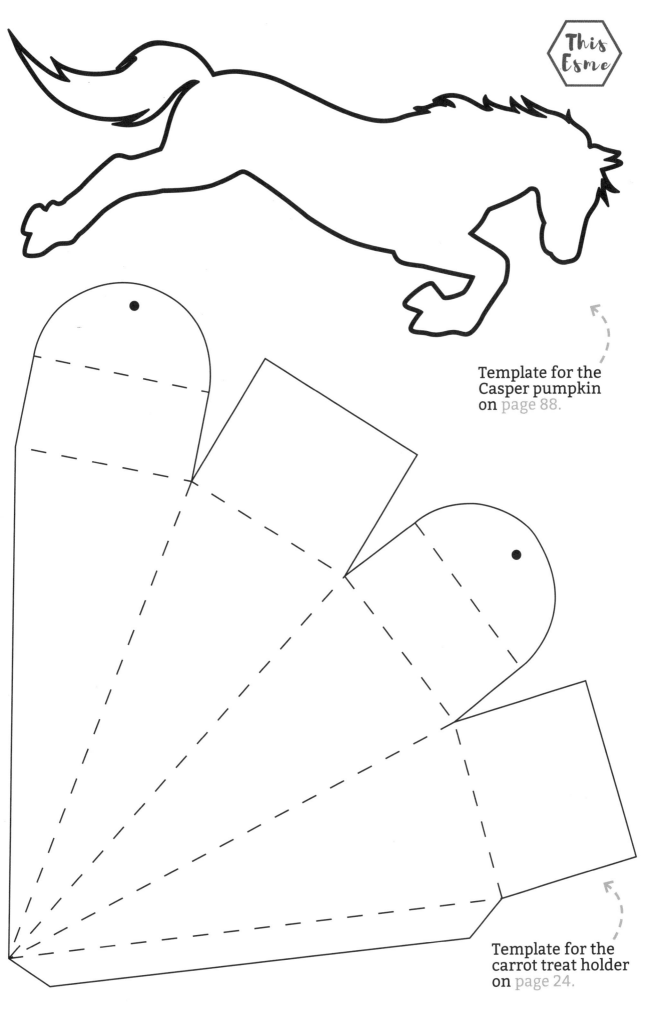

Template for the
Casper pumpkin
on page 88.

Template for the
carrot treat holder
on page 24.

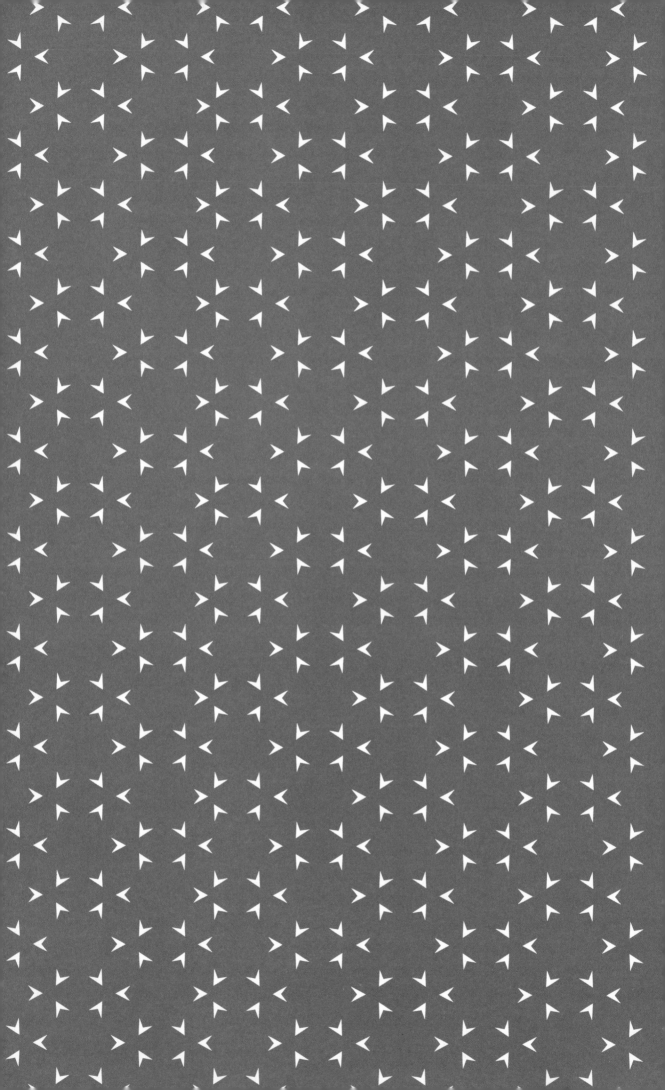